Core Knowledge Language Arts®

What's in Our Universe?

Unit 7 Reader

Skills Strand
GRADE 3

Amplify learning.

Core Knowledge®

Table of Contents
What's in Our Universe?
Unit 7 Reader

Pausing Point (Additional Chapters for Enrichment)

The Sun, Earth, and Our Solar System

Chapter

1

Look up in the sky at noon. What do you see? If it is not cloudy, you will see the sun shining brightly in the sky.

The sun provides energy—both light and heat energy. The sun's light and heat give life to plants and animals. Without the sun, Earth would be freezing cold. Have you ever wondered what the sun is made of or why it gives off so much light and heat?

The sun gives us light and heat energy.

You may be surprised to know that the sun is a star. It is in fact the closest star to Earth. It is made up of different, hot gases. How hot? A hot summer day on Earth is 100 degrees. On the sun, it is 10,000 degrees! The sun stays that hot all the time! The sun's gases create the light and heat energy it gives off.

Long ago, people believed that the sun moved around Earth. This seemed to make sense. Each morning at the start of the day, the sun rose in the east. At the end of the day, the sun set in the west—exactly opposite from where it had came up. To explain this change, people said the sun moved around Earth. But now we know that this is not what really happens. The sun does not move around Earth. It is Earth that moves around the sun!

A close-up of the sun

The sun is in the center of a group of eight **planets**. All of these **planets**, including Earth, circle, or **orbit**, around the sun. The sun, **planets**, and other objects in space that **orbit** the sun are called the **solar system**. The word *solar* has the Latin root word *sol*, which means "the sun." Everything in the **solar system** relates to the sun.

Planets orbiting *the sun*

Our **planet**, Earth, moves in two ways. We have just learned that Earth circles around the sun. It takes about 365 days, which is one year, for Earth to **orbit** the sun.

Earth also moves by spinning, or **rotating**, on its **axis**. It is this spinning that makes day and night on Earth and the motion of the sun across the sky from sunrise to sunset. It takes one day for Earth to make one complete **rotation** on its axis. As Earth **rotates** and spins, different parts of it face the sun. When the part facing the sun gets sunlight, it is daytime on that side of Earth. The part that faces away from the sun gets no sunlight. So, on that side of Earth, it is nighttime. Did you know that when it is daytime where we live, it is nighttime on the other side of Earth?

*Earth spins on its **axis**. On the side of Earth facing the sun, it is daytime. On the side facing away from the sun, it is nighttime.*

When Earth **rotates** on its **axis**, it is **tilted**. At certain times of the year, one part of Earth is **tilted** toward the sun. The sunlight is more direct and it feels hotter. For people living on this part of Earth, it is summer. For people living on the part of Earth **tilted** away from the sun, there is less sunlight and it is winter. So, when it is summertime for us, there are people living on other parts of Earth where it is winter! So, the fact that Earth is **tilted** on its **axis** is what creates the seasons of the year.

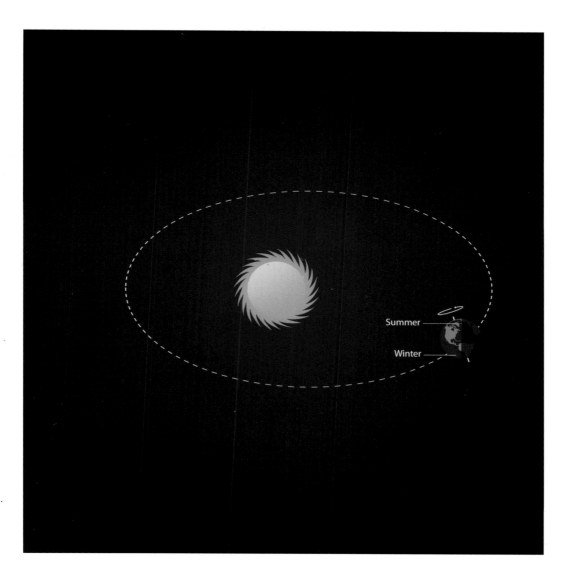

Summer

Winter

*When Earth is **tilted** on its **axis** towards the sun, it is spring and summer. When Earth is **tilted** on its **axis** away from the sun, it is fall and winter.*

2 The Moon

Look up in the sky at night. What do you see? If it is not cloudy, you may be able to see the moon.

When you see the moon at night, it might look white. It might look gray or silver. Sometimes, it seems to shine and glow. But the moon does not give off light the way the sun does. The moon is a ball of rock that gives off no light of its own. It simply reflects light from the sun. That means light from the sun hits the moon and bounces off.

Our moon is easily visible on most clear nights.

You already know that Earth orbits around the sun. But did you know that the moon orbits around Earth? It takes just about one month for the moon to completely circle Earth. If you look up at the night sky each night of the month, you may think that the size and shape of the moon is changing. However, the size and shape are not really changing. The moon is still a round ball. It looks different at different times of the month because of the way the light from the sun is reflected and how much of the moon we can see from Earth.

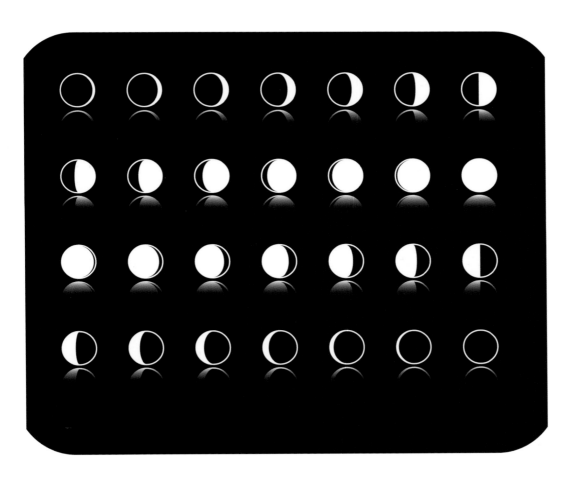

This chart shows the phases of the moon. It shows what you might see if you looked at the moon each night for a month. You can read the chart just like you would read a book. Start at the top and go from left to right. When you finish reading the first row, go on to the next one. You can see how the moon seems to change during the month.

The way that Earth, the moon, and the sun move can also make other interesting things to look at in the sky. When Earth, the moon, and the sun all move together in a direct line, something called an **eclipse** can take place.

We can see two kinds of **eclipses** from Earth. One kind happens when the moon gets in between the sun and Earth. When that happens, we can't see the sun for a while. At least, we can't see part of it. We call this a solar **eclipse** or an **eclipse** of the sun.

*During an **eclipse** of the sun, the moon moves between Earth and sun and blocks out the sun.*

The other kind of **eclipse**, called a lunar eclipse, also involves the sun, the moon, and Earth. It takes place when the moon passes behind Earth and into its shadow. In the image on the next page, you can see that a shadow covers part of the moon. It is Earth's shadow that you see. Earth has blocked out the sun and left part of the moon in darkness.

Eclipses do not happen often because the sun, Earth, and the moon all have to line up just right. Solar **eclipses** can only be seen from a narrow strip of Earth at a time. While they happen once or twice a year, it is very, very rare to see one. **Eclipses** of the moon happen more often, several times each year. They can be seen from half of Earth at a time, so are more often visible.

Whether or not you can see an **eclipse** depends on where you are on Earth. You must never look directly at a solar **eclipse**. The sun is very bright and could burn your eyes. But, it is safe to look at an **eclipse** of the moon. If an **eclipse** is predicted, it is usually big news, so you will likely hear about it.

What's in Our Universe?

*The moon during a lunar **eclipse***

The Planets
Closest to the Sun:
Mercury, Venus, Earth, and Mars

Our planet Earth is one of eight planets in our solar system that orbit around the sun. The other planets are Mercury, Venus, Mars, Jupiter, Saturn, Uranus, and Neptune. People have been looking at the planets for thousands of years. People from Mesopotamia, the Greeks, Mayans, Incas, and Aztecs were all interested in the planets. They used just their **naked eye** to study the planets. Now, we have telescopes and other tools that help us get a better look at the planets.

A telescope

The four planets closest to the sun—
Mercury, Venus, Earth, and Mars—are small
planets. These planets have a rocky, or solid,
surface.

Mercury and Venus are closer to the sun than
Earth. The other planets are farther away.

Earth needs 365 days to make one orbit
around the sun. That is the length of one year
on Earth.

The closer a planet is to the sun, the less
time it needs to make an orbit around the sun.
Mercury is the closest planet to the sun. It needs
just 88 days to make one orbit. Venus is the
next closest to the sun. It needs just 225 days to
make an orbit. The planets that are farther away
take much longer. It takes Neptune 165 years to
orbit the sun!

Mercury

Venus

Earth

Mars

The sun and planets

Besides being closest to the sun, Mercury is the smallest of all the planets. The English name for the planet comes from the Romans. They named the planet after the Roman god Mercury. The Greek name for this same god is Hermes.

Venus is the second planet from the sun and is closest to Earth. This planet was named after the Roman goddess of love. For a long time, scientists thought that Venus might be a lot like Earth. After all, it is close to Earth. It is about the same size as Earth and it is covered with clouds, like Earth. But this idea turned out to be wrong, too. We know now that Venus and Earth are different in lots of ways.

Scientists had to change their ideas to fit the new facts. They have now concluded that Venus is much hotter than Earth. It would not be a good place for us to live or even visit.

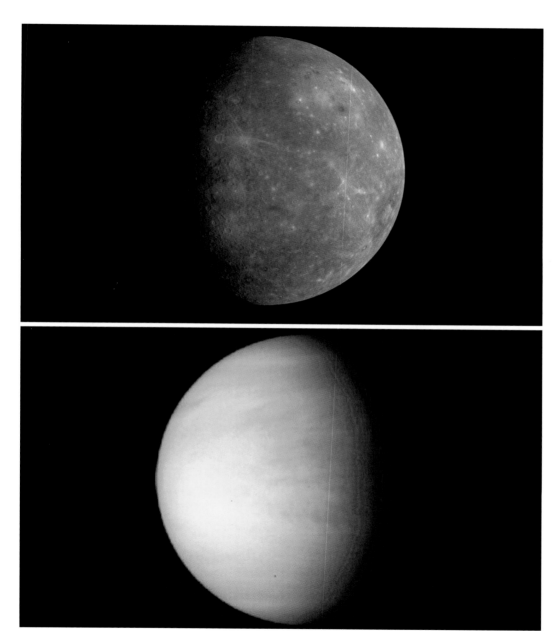

Mercury (top) and Venus

Mars is the fourth planet from the sun. It is named after the Roman god of war. When you look at Mars in the night sky, it looks quite red. This is because the rocks on Mars contain rust.

Many space **probes** and robots have landed on Mars. They have taken photographs and also dug up rocks.

One **probe** that went to Mars not long ago found some ice. That was big news. Ice is frozen water. If there is water on Mars, there might be life. Some experts argue that nothing could live on Mars. They say it is too cold and too dry. Others think there might be life on Mars. They think there might be something alive down under the rocks. Still others think there might have been life on Mars at one time but there isn't any now.

Mars

Chapter 4 The Outer Planets: Jupiter, Saturn, Uranus, and Neptune

Do you remember the names of the four planets closest to the sun? If you said, "Mercury, Venus, Earth, and Mars," you are right! There are four more planets called the outer planets. So there are eight planets in all.

Jupiter is the very next planet after Mars. After Jupiter come Saturn, Uranus, and Neptune in that order. Neptune is the planet that is farthest from the sun. Uranus is difficult to see with the naked eye and Neptune is impossible to see without help. Neptune is only visible using a telescope.

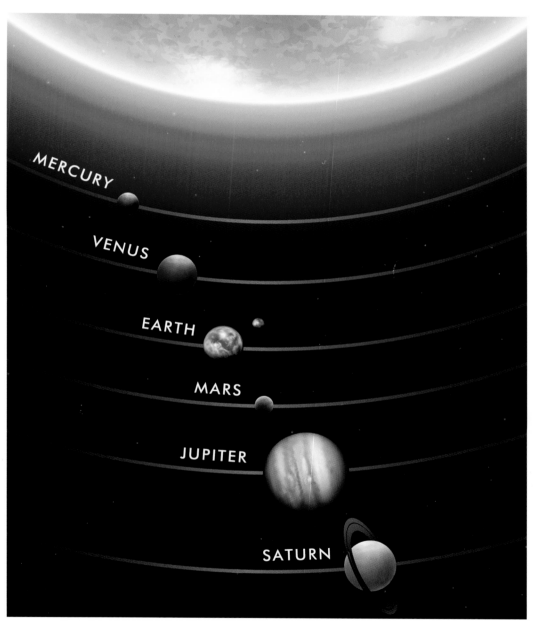

MERCURY

VENUS

EARTH

MARS

JUPITER

SATURN

Our solar system: the sun and eight planets

The outer planets are very large and are mostly made of gas. Scientists often call these planets **gas giants**. Of all the planets, Jupiter is the largest: 1,300 Earths could fit inside Jupiter! It is made mostly of **hydrogen** gas, the most common gas in the universe.

The gases on Jupiter seem to be blowing around. In the image of Jupiter on the next page, you can see the giant, red spot. It looks like an eye! Experts think it is a big wind storm, like a huge hurricane.

Jupiter also has 63 known moons that orbit it. Some of these moons are very large, even larger than Earth's moon.

Jupiter and some of its moons

Saturn is known for its many large rings that orbit the planet. These rings are made of ice and dust. The ice reflects light and makes the rings glow. Saturn also has many moons that orbit it.

Saturn and its rings

The last two planets are Uranus and Neptune. These planets are the farthest from the sun so they are very cold. Uranus and Neptune also have rings, but they aren't easily seen like Saturn's. Both planets also have moons.

So now you know the names of all eight planets. Try asking the adults in your family how many planets there are. They may tell you that there are nine planets. When the adults in your family were in school, people said that there was a ninth planet called Pluto. But in 2006, scientists decided that Pluto did not have all of the characteristics needed to be classified as a planet. They removed Pluto's name from the list of planets, so now there are only eight planets.

This is Neptune as it might look if seen from one of its moons. The shadow of another moon makes a dark spot on the planet's surface.

Chapter 5
Asteroids, Comets, and Meteors

There are other objects that orbit the sun in the solar system besides the planets. Millions of space rocks called **asteroids** also orbit the sun. **Asteroids** are made of rock, metal, and sometimes ice. Many **asteroids** are found orbiting the sun between the planets Mars and Jupiter. They cluster together in a shape like a belt as they orbit the sun. This part of the solar system is called the **asteroid belt**.

*Top: An artist's image of an **asteroid belt** around a star*
*Bottom: An up-close image of an **asteroid** from our solar system*

Comets also orbit the sun. **Comets** are made mostly of ice and dust. When a **comet** gets close to the sun, the sun's heat causes some of the **comet** to change into a gas. This gas streams off the end of the **comet** like a tail.

The most famous **comet** is **Halley's Comet**. It is named for the British scientist Edmund Halley who first discovered it. **Halley's Comet** is visible from Earth with the naked eye every 76 years. It was last seen in 1986. Can you figure out when it will be seen again?

*A **comet** in the night sky*

Other kinds of space rocks called **meteoroids** are also found throughout the solar system. When a **meteoroid** enters Earth's **atmosphere**, we call it a **meteor**. Small pieces of the **meteor** burn brightly and look like a white trail across the sky when viewed from Earth. Sometimes people call this a "shooting star." Have you ever seen one? A **meteor** "shower" is when many **meteors** can be seen falling in the sky on the same night. Sometimes they last over several nights. It's an amazing space show!

If a **meteor** doesn't fully burn up in the **atmosphere**, it falls to Earth and can make a large hole called a crater. Pieces of a meteor found on the ground are **meteorites**.

*An artist's drawing of a **meteor** shower at night*

***Meteor** Crater in Arizona formed when a **meteorite** hit Earth. Notice the road and buildings to the left of the crater. This crater is very big!*

6 Galaxies and Stars

Look up in the sky at night. What do you see besides the moon? If it is not cloudy, you may be able to see lots of stars glittering in the sky.

Remember that the sun is also a star. The stars in the night sky do not look like the sun. They do not look as big or as bright. But they are, in fact, very much alike. The stars in the night sky are big balls of hot gas, just like the sun.

So why don't they look the same? The night stars are much, much farther away from Earth than the sun. That is why they look like tiny specks of light. If we could get close to the stars, they would look bigger, brighter, and more like the sun. But the stars we see at night are so far away that no one from Earth has ever been able to get close to them.

Stars in the night sky

Scientists who study the stars and outer space are called **astronomers**. The Greek root word *astron* means star. The prefix *astro* is used in many other English words.

All stars are big balls of hot gas, but **astronomers** have discovered that stars differ in many ways. Stars can be different sizes and colors. Some stars are closer to Earth than others and some stars are hotter than others. Stars that are the hottest and closest to Earth appear brighter than other stars.

All stars are made of gases, but they can differ in size, color, and brightness.

Astronomers also discovered that stars cluster together in large groups. A large group of stars that cluster together in one area is called a **galaxy**. There are **billions** and **billions** of stars in one **galaxy**. That's a lot of stars!

The **galaxy** to which our sun and solar system belong is called the **Milky Way Galaxy**. It has a spiral shape when viewed from space. From Earth, it looks like a "milky" band of white light.

*The **Milky Way** as it appears in the night sky*

The nearest spiral galaxy to the **Milky Way Galaxy** is called the **Andromeda Galaxy**. It is **billions** and **billions** of miles from the **Milky Way Galaxy**. There's that number **billions** again. You have probably heard of a million before. A million is a huge number. So what's a **billion**? It's one thousand million! It is safe to say that the **Andromeda Galaxy** is a long, long, long way away! Even so, it is sometimes possible to see the **Andromeda Galaxy** at night.

Scientists think there are **billions** of **galaxies** in the universe. There's that number **billions** again. There are **billions** of stars in each **galaxy** and **billions** of **galaxies** in the universe—that is almost more than you can think about!

Andromeda Galaxy

Chapter 7

Constellations

Go outside one night and look at the stars. Of the billions of stars in our galaxy, it is possible to see only 2,000 with the naked eye. When you first look at them, you might not see much. They might look like just a bunch of tiny dots.

Look a little closer. You will see that some stars shine more brightly than others. Focus on the bright stars. Which ones really jump out at you?

Then, focus on the spaces in between the bright stars. Ask yourself, "What would it look like if I drew lines from one bright star to the next? What would it look like if I were to connect the dots? Would I see any shapes? Would I see any patterns?"

Since ancient times, people have been studying the stars. When ancient people looked at the stars, some seemed to be closer together and formed patterns.

On a clear night away from city lights, you can see the stars that fill the night sky.

One of the first people to describe these star patterns, called constellations, was a man named Ptolemy [TO-lə-mee]. He picked out the brightest stars and traced lines from one star to the next. He saw all types of shapes and patterns. One looked like a bull. He saw another that looked like a crab. A third looked like a bear. In all, he found 48 constellations. Much later, 40 more constellations were added to Ptolemy's list. Today, astronomers say there are 88 constellations that can be seen in the night sky.

On the next page is a drawing of a **constellation** that Ptolemy described. It is called **Ursa Major** or Big Bear. The white dots or circles stand for the stars in the **constellation**. The dotted lines connect the stars and trace the pattern so you can see the shape. Do you see a Big Bear in the pattern? It does not look exactly like a real bear. So, you may need to **imagine** that it looks like a bear. Hint: its head is to the left with its nose being the star that is on the far left.

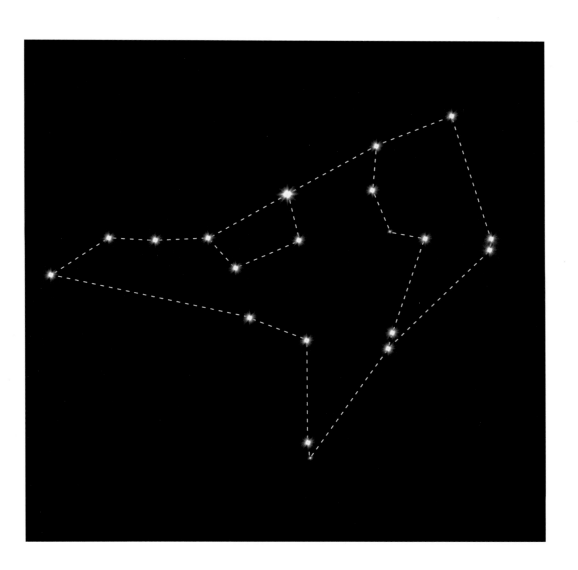

Ursa Major

Within **Ursa Major**, there are seven very bright stars that form another small group of stars called the Big Dipper. Look at the image at the top of the next page. Can you see why it is called the Big Dipper? When you trace a line from star to star, the shape looks like a dipper. A dipper is like a ladle you can use to scoop something into a bowl. The stars on the left look like the handle. The stars on the right look like the scoop.

Ptolemy also described another **constellation** called **Ursa Minor** or Little Bear. This **constellation** is also made up of seven stars. In the image on the bottom of the next page, the seven dots stand for the stars. An artist has added a drawing of a bear to help you better **imagine** how the star pattern looks like a bear.

The Big Dipper

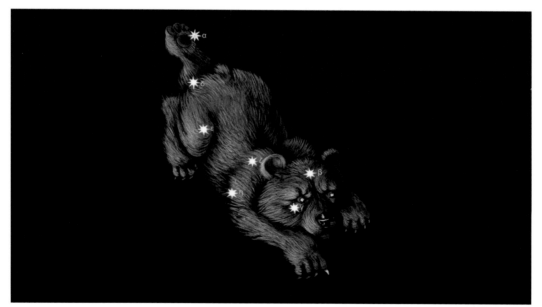

Ursa Minor

Ursa Minor is also called the Little Dipper. The brightest star at the end of the handle is called **Polaris**. Can you see it? **Polaris** stays in the same place in the night sky all year long. (Other stars are found in different places in the sky at different times of the year.) **Polaris's** place in the sky is almost directly over the North Pole of Earth. By finding **Polaris**, also called the North Star, you can find the direction north and the other directions. In ancient times, sailors and explorers used this star to find their way when they traveled.

Try to find **Polaris** the next time you look at the night sky. Start by first looking for the Big Dipper because it is easier to find. Then, find the two "pointer" stars at the edge of the Big Dipper's scoop. Then, pretend there is a long arrow pointing the same way as the pointer stars. The first star you will see at the end of the arrow is **Polaris**.

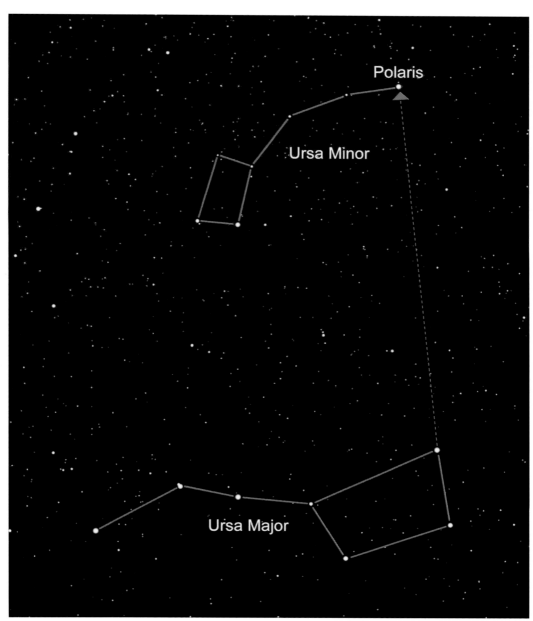

*The 'pointer' stars of the Big Dipper pointing to **Polaris**, the North Star*

8 Exploring Space

As you have learned in the last chapters, people have been interested in studying space since ancient times. It was possible to see only some stars and planets with the naked eye. Since they were far, far away, it was impossible to see anything in very much detail.

In 1609, an astronomer named Galileo [ga-li-LAE-oe] created a telescope that he used to observe the night sky. Galileo's telescope made things appear three times larger. Using his telescope, he discovered four of the many moons that orbit the planet Jupiter. He also observed the planet Saturn and the Milky Way.

A portrait of Galileo holding a telescope

Since Galileo's time, scientists have created more and more powerful telescopes. Some telescopes are housed in large **observatories** on Earth. Often, these **observatories** are on the top of mountains, far away from any cities or lights. This allows astronomers to clearly see the stars and planets.

*Building an **observatory** on top of a mountain helps to get a better view of the sky.*

Other telescopes are **launched** into space using rockets. They travel far above Earth and have a better view of the universe than telescopes on Earth. One of these telescopes is the **Hubble Telescope**. It was launched in 1990 by **NASA**, the American group of scientists who study outer space. The **Hubble Telescope** is still in space today, orbiting Earth. Since its **launch**, it has sent back thousands of photos to **NASA**. **Hubble's** photos have led to many new discoveries about the universe. For example, using photos from **Hubble**, scientists now think that the universe is about 13 to 14 billion years old!

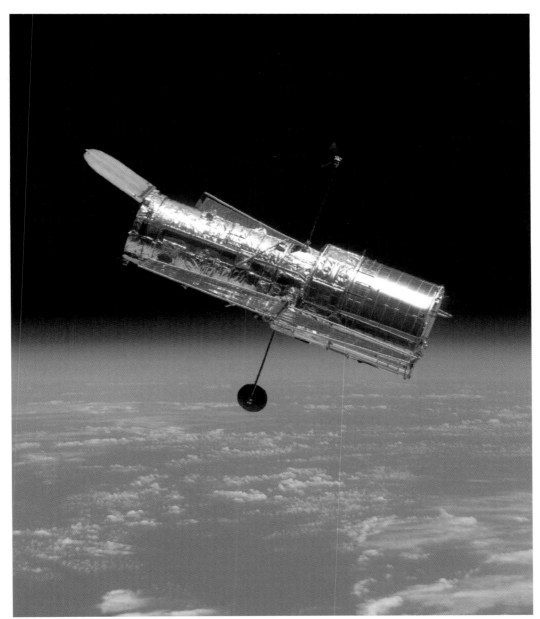

*The **Hubble Telescope** orbits Earth above its atmosphere.*

Besides sending telescopes into space, **NASA** has also launched rocket ships into space. Scientists believed it was too dangerous for humans to ride the first rocket ships into space. They did not know what effects space travel might have on humans. So, **NASA** first sent apes into space on rocket ships. "Why apes?" you might ask. Think back to what you learned in a previous reader about animals. Apes are mammals and belong to the same group of animals, called primates, as humans. By studying the apes, scientists hoped to learn how space travel might affect humans. In 1961, **NASA** sent the first American **astronaut** into space on a rocket ship. His name was Alan Shepard. He stayed in space for only 15 minutes.

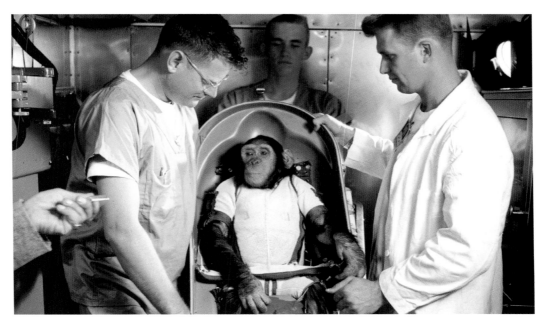

Top image: Ham, one of the first apes **launched** into space
Bottom image: Alan Shepard was the first American **astronaut** in space.

After 1961, **NASA** sent more **manned** flights into space. These flights orbited Earth but did not stop or land anywhere in space. Then, in 1969, the United States sent a rocket ship to the moon. The rocket ship was called **Apollo 11**.

Apollo 11 *fires its rockets during lift-off.*

Have you ever tried to throw a ball up in the air? The ball goes up at first. Then, it comes back down. No matter how hard you throw it, it comes back down because of **gravity**. **Gravity** is a force of **attraction** that pulls things toward one another. Earth's **gravity** pulls the ball back down to Earth.

Earth's **gravity** is a challenge for rocket ships like **Apollo 11**. In order to fly off into outer space, the rocket ship has to push up with a lot of force. It has to push up with so much force that **gravity** cannot pull it back down.

Apollo 11 fired a lot of strong rockets. It lifted off and went up slowly at first. Then, it got faster and faster. This is what it looked like after a few seconds. After just a few seconds more, it shot up out of Earth's atmosphere and into outer space.

Apollo 11 *shooting up into space*

9 A Walk on the Moon

Once Apollo 11 was up in space, the astronauts had to steer it to the moon. There were three astronauts on Apollo 11. You can see them in the image on the next page. Each had a job to do. One of them was in charge of flying the spaceship, called Columbia. The other two had to get into a landing craft called the Eagle. Then, they had to steer it down and land it on the moon.

The Apollo 11 astronauts

The astronaut who had to steer the Eagle was named Neil Armstrong. He had to find a good, flat spot to land. He also had to set the Eagle down gently.

Lots of people tuned in to watch Armstrong and the Eagle on live TV. At first, Armstrong had a hard time getting the Eagle to go where he wanted it to go. But, in the end, he landed it just fine.

Armstrong sent a message back by radio: "The Eagle has landed!"

The crowds watching it on TV went wild. They danced and sang. They shouted and waved the United States flag. For the first time ever, humans had landed on the moon!

What happened next was even more amazing. The astronauts went for a walk on the moon!

Here is one of the Apollo 11 astronauts walking on the moon. Can you see his footprints?

There is no air for breathing on the moon. It is also very cold. So, the astronauts could not just walk out in shorts and a T-shirt. They had to put on space suits like the one in the image on the next page. They had to wear masks. They had to carry tanks full of air for breathing.

Armstrong went out first. He went down the steps of the Eagle until he was on the last one. Then, he made a little hop. He landed on the moon and kicked up a little moon dust. Then, he said, "That's one small step for man, one giant leap for mankind." Another astronaut joined Armstrong on the moon. His name was Buzz Aldrin.

Once again, people watching it on TV cheered. They were proud that the United States had put a man on the moon!

Buzz Aldrin plants the U.S. flag on the moon.

While Armstrong and Aldrin were on the moon, pilot Michael Collins stayed on a part of the spaceship that was still orbiting the moon. Armstrong and Aldrin spent more than 21 hours on the moon. They found that it was easy to move about on the moon, which has less gravity than Earth. They could jump up high and seemed to float down slowly. They used different tools to explore the moon. They knew the scientists back on Earth were hoping to learn new information about the moon. They dug up samples of moon rocks to take back to Earth.

After exploring the moon, Aldrin and Armstrong got back in the Eagle. They lifted off. They met up with Michael Collins on board the other part of the spaceship. Then, all three of them flew back to Earth. The spaceship came speeding back from space and splashed down into the sea. A Navy ship came to pick up the astronauts and take them back to NASA.

Splashdown of Apollo 11

Chapter 10
What's it Like in Space?

Since Apollo 11, many more astronauts have traveled in space. Scientists have learned that there are many differences between Earth and space. One of the biggest differences has to do with gravity. Remember that gravity is a force of attraction that pulls things toward one another. The force of gravity on Earth is pretty strong. Even the best jumpers can only jump a few feet off the ground. (Try it and see!)

Want to jump high? You will have to fight against gravity.

Remember that on the moon, astronauts Aldrin and Armstrong were easily able to jump up high. They didn't come down quickly either. Instead, they seemed to float down slowly. That was because the force of gravity on the moon is not as strong as on Earth. The moon is not as big as Earth. So the force of gravity is not as strong on the moon.

If you think that is cool, wait until you read what happens out in space, away from the moon or planets. Out in space, astronauts do not feel the effects of gravity. They and their spaceship are moving freely in space. Since the astronaut and spaceship are moving freely together, the astronauts look and feel as if they are floating!

This astronaut is inside a spaceship in space, where the force of gravity is less.

Up in space, lots of things are different. You can do a flip and not worry about whether you will make it all the way around before you come down!

When you are free of the effects of gravity, it is easier to do flips and cartwheels.

Eating is different in space, too. I'll bet when you eat lunch at school, your food stays where you put it. If you set it on a table, it stays there until you pick it up. The force of gravity holds it down. But if you were up in space, you and your food would be moving freely together. If you let go of it, your food might drift away!

Look, no hands! These astronauts' lunches appear to be floating!

There are other differences in space besides less gravity. Do you remember that the astronauts on the moon had to carry tanks of air for breathing? Another way outer space is different from Earth is that there is no air or oxygen at all in outer space. Look again at the image on page 87 of the astronauts inside the spaceship. The astronauts are not carrying tanks of air. That's because oxygen is being pumped inside the spaceship.

Since there is no air in space, you also do not hear sounds in outer space. It is also very cold in space. The astronauts must train many months before going into space so they know what to expect. Do you think you would like to go into space some day?

This is what Earth looks like from the moon. Can you name some ways that being in space is different from being on Earth?

Chapter 11 The Space Shuttle

Interest in manned space **exploration** soared after Apollo 11. Other astronauts went to the moon. But scientists were also interested in exploring other parts of space beyond the moon. It was very expensive and took a lot of time to build and send spaceships into space. Do you remember that when Apollo 11 returned from space, it landed in the sea? It was not able to land safely on the ground, so this type of spacecraft always had to land in the sea. Once it landed in the sea, this kind of spacecraft could not be used again.

In 1981, a **reusable** spacecraft, called a **space shuttle**, was built. It was able to fly up into space and then zoom back down to Earth. When it returned to Earth, the pilot was able to land the spacecraft on a runway almost like an airplane. It glided down from space and landed on a runway, but it had to be a very long runway.

*A **space shuttle** lifts off*

The **space shuttle** was flown back into space again and again. It **shuttled** back and forth between Earth and space. That is why it was called the **space shuttle**.

The image on the previous page shows the launch of a **space shuttle**. The **space shuttle** itself is the white part that looks like a jet plane. The other parts are **booster rockets**. The **booster rockets** helped the **space shuttle** get off the ground. They helped the **space shuttle** overcome Earth's gravity. Once the **space shuttle** was up into space, it dropped the **booster rockets** because it no longer needed them.

*A **space shuttle** in orbit above Earth*

In the thirty years between 1981 and 2011, different **space shuttles** carried astronauts up into space on many missions. The **space shuttle** was also used to bring **research** equipment and tools into space. The astronauts did many experiments to find out more about space. Scientists were **especially** interested in learning about what effect the lack of gravity would have on humans and other living things.

The **space shuttle** was also used to help build an amazing **space station**. Astronauts could live at the **space station** for months at a time. Often, the **space shuttle** carried supplies back and forth from Earth to the **space station**. It also provided a ride home to Earth when it was time for the astronauts to return.

The last **space shuttle** mission took place in July 2011. NASA scientists and Americans were proud of everything the astronauts had accomplished in thirty years. With the end of the **space shuttle** missions, NASA is planning other ways to explore space. Those plans include launching **unmanned** probes and **satellites**. NASA scientists hope to learn more about the moon's gravity and are even talking about trying to explore asteroids!

*A **space shuttle** comes in for a landing.*

Chapter 12 The International Space Station

Would you like to have a bedroom in outer space? Some astronauts do!

The United States and other countries use the space shuttle to send astronauts to an **international** space station. The space station orbits Earth. Three astronauts can live there at one time. They stay for six months at a time. This image shows the space station.

The space station orbits Earth.

The space station orbits far above Earth. So the astronauts in the space station don't feel the effects of gravity like we do on Earth. When we lift our arms and legs here on Earth, we have to work against gravity. That is good for us. It helps us stay in shape. But astronauts in space don't have the effects of gravity to work against. They do not get much of a workout from drifting around. They have to run at least once a day to stay in good shape. In this image, you can see an astronaut jogging in space.

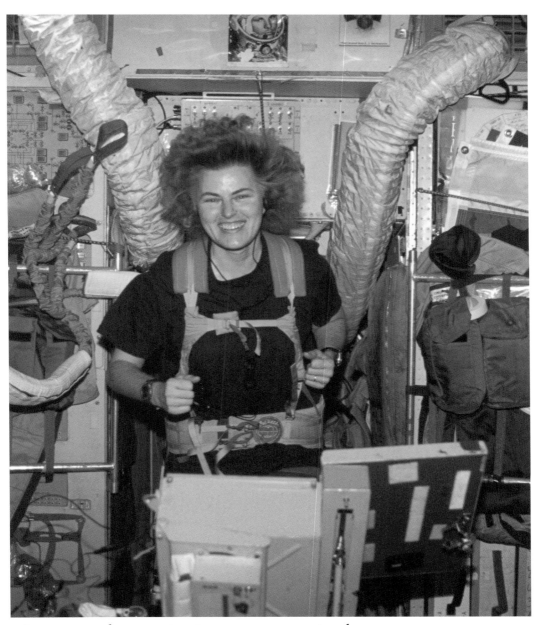

Astronauts have to jog in space to stay in shape.

These two men are sleeping in space. They don't feel the effects of gravity so they are moving freely within the spaceship. This means they can sleep right side up or upside down. It is all the same. Do you think you would like sleeping this way?

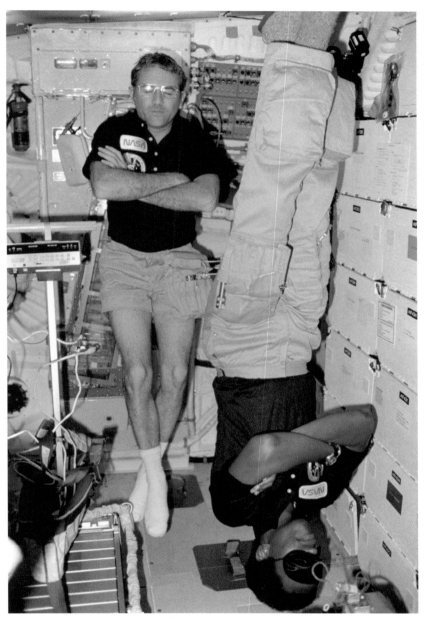

These two astronauts are taking a nap in space.

Taking a shower in space is tricky. On Earth, the water comes out of the spout. It falls down and splashes on your body. Then, it runs off. But this is not what happens in space! In space, you have to rub the water on your skin. Also, it does not just drip off. You have to scrape it off. You have to shower in a little pod. The pod keeps the water you scrape off your skin from drifting off in the air. If it drifted off, it might cause problems. It might mess up the computers and equipment inside the space station.

You can see that lots of things are different when you live in space. That is why leaving the space station and coming back to Earth can be hard. It takes time for the astronauts to get used to Earth again. After months in space, they struggle with the gravity on Earth. Their arms and legs feel heavy. They find it hard to stand up. They feel off balance. But in a few weeks, they begin to feel normal again. Sometimes when they look up at the sky, they even feel a little homesick for their home in outer space.

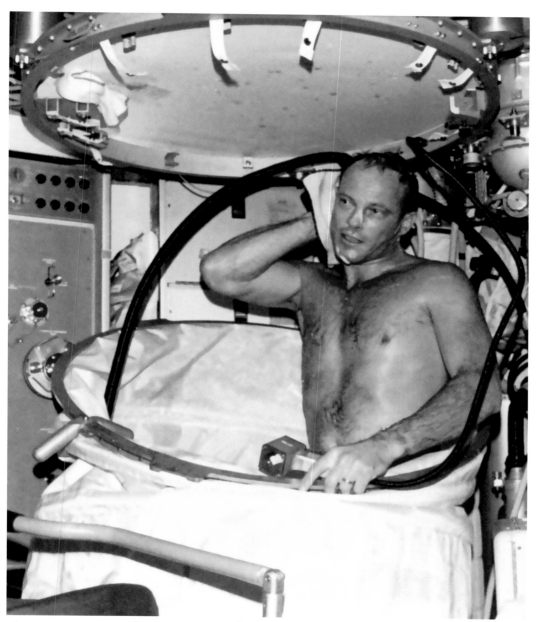

An astronaut taking a space shower

Chapter 13 Dr. Mae Jemison

Do you know what a role model is? A role model is someone who sets an example for others by the way he or she lives. Many students admire people who are famous athletes, movie stars, or singers and use them as role models. They see them on TV, in newspapers and in magazines, and decide they want to be like them. But some of the best role models are people that you probably would not see on TV or in newspapers. They have jobs such as doctors, teachers, or policemen. Some are scientists and astronauts. One such person is Mae Jemison.

Mae Jemison

Mae Jemison was born October 17, 1956, in Decatur, Alabama. Her family moved to Chicago, Illinois when she was young. Mae always took great pride in her schoolwork. She was interested in science, but was also interested in the arts. She finished high school early at age 16! From there, she went to Stanford University in California. Most college students focus on only one topic of study because college is so challenging. Mae focused and excelled in two topics of study—**chemical engineering** and **African-American studies**!

After Stanford, Mae entered medical school to become a doctor. She wanted to use her medical training to help people in Africa and countries where people were poor. So, she joined the **Peace Corps** as a **volunteer**. **Health care** in Africa was often not very good. Mae treated patients and also helped train other **health care** workers. She worked hard to help improve **health care** in the countries where she worked.

Stanford University, where Mae went to college

After the **Peace Corps**, Mae came back to the United States. She set her sights on a different goal. Her greatest dream was to become an astronaut and travel into space. She decided to apply to NASA to become an astronaut. But the first time she applied, she was not accepted. Instead of giving up, she tried again and NASA accepted her the second time! She was one of only 15 people chosen from a group of 2,000 people who wanted to become astronauts!

Her training to become an astronaut was hard. She had to get into great shape and train to get used to being free of the effects of gravity in space. She also had to study and pass many tests about space travel. Mae Jemison succeeded in both.

*An experiment studying the effects of **weightlessness***

In 1992, Mae was chosen for a mission on the *Endeavour* space shuttle. A rocket launched the *Endeavour* into orbit around Earth. Mae became the first African-American female astronaut in space!

The mission was to study the effects of **weightlessness** on plants and animals. Mae conducted experiments during the mission with fellow astronaut Jan Davis. They collected information that the scientists at NASA could study. The mission was a great success.

After her successful mission, Mae retired from NASA. She became a professor at Dartmouth College, sharing her love of science and space with other students. She also started her own company called The Jemison Group, Inc. Mae's company continues to work with people in poor countries, searching for ways that science can help improve these people's lives. Mae Jemison is truly a role model that we can all admire!

Mae Jemison achieves her goal of becoming an astronaut.

Chapter 14
Nicolaus Copernicus

Do you remember in the very first chapter of this reader you learned that long ago, people believed that the sun moved around Earth? This seemed to make sense. Each morning at the start of the day, the sun rose in the east. At the end of the day, the sun set in the west—exactly opposite from where it had come up. To explain this change, people said the sun moved around Earth. This is what the Greeks and other ancient people believed. But you also learned in the first chapter that this was not true.

About the same time that Christopher Columbus arrived in America, a man named Nicolaus Copernicus was studying math and astronomy at a university in Poland. He later moved to Italy where he also studied medicine and law.

Young Copernicus studied math, astronomy, medicine, and law.

But Copernicus' real love was astronomy. He knew that since ancient times, people believed that the sun moved around Earth. Copernicus began to carefully observe and record the movement of the sun, planets, and stars. After much research, Copernicus decided that the belief that the sun moved around Earth could not be true. Copernicus' observations led him to believe just the opposite! He realized that instead, Earth was moving around the sun! He also believed that as Earth orbited the sun, it also completed a full rotation each day.

All of Copernicus' ideas came from viewing space without the help of a telescope. He wrote down what he observed from a cathedral bell tower. He also used math to help him prove his point. Finally, Copernicus wrote a book explaining his new ideas about how the universe worked. His fellow scientists went to work trying to prove him wrong, but they couldn't. Most were amazed by his discovery!

What's in Our Universe?

Copernicus spent hours observing the movement of the stars, planets, and sun.

However, Copernicus' ideas were different from what people had believed for thousands of years. They believed that Earth and humans were the center of the universe. Many of the teachings of the church at that time were also based on this belief. Copernicus had dared to suggest that Earth was not the center of the universe. Instead, he said, the sun was at the center! Many in the church disagreed with Copernicus' ideas and spoke out against them. So, his beliefs were not widely accepted while he was alive.

In fact, even after Copernicus died, the church continued to argue against the view that the sun was at the center of the universe. Some scientists agreed with Copernicus' ideas. Galileo agreed with Copernicus and was punished and put in jail for a long time.

Today we know, of course, that Copernicus was right. It took great **courage** to speak up and suggest an idea that was so different from what people had always believed. But that is how science works. Even today, scientists continue to learn new things about the universe, so our knowledge is always changing and growing.

What's in Our Universe?

Copernicus argued that the sun, not Earth, was at the center of the universe.

Chapter 15 The Big Bang

Have you ever wondered how the universe and our solar system came to be? Astronomers have studied the universe for thousands of years. During that time, people suggested many different explanations of how our solar system began.

With the help of telescopes, modern astronomers noticed that all of the distant galaxies in the universe seem to be moving outward. The more distant the galaxies, the faster they are moving outward. Stars are moving away from Earth and so are whole galaxies. In 1929, a scientist named Edwin Hubble discovered this distance versus speed that is now called "Hubble's Law." (This is the same "Hubble" after whom the Hubble Telescope is named!)

Edwin Hubble discovered that all the distant galaxies in the universe seem to be moving outward.

Hubble's observation led scientists to offer explanations of how the solar system started. There are many explanations, or **theories**, about how the universe came to be. One recent **theory** or idea is known as the **Big Bang Theory**. A **theory** in science tries to explain how something happened or how something works.

Three **astrophysicists** proposed the **Big Bang Theory** in the 1960s. **Astrophysicists** are scientists who use math to study the universe. George Lemaitre, Alexander Friedmann, and Edwin Hubble studied the theories of another scientist by the name of Albert Einstein. They used his ideas to develop their explanation of how the universe first started.

*Many **astrophysicists** contributed to the development of the **Big Bang Theory**.*

They suggested that long ago, the universe and everything in it was once a tiny ball. All of the stuff that makes the universe (called **matter**) was squeezed together into one tiny space. Imagine if all the planets and all the stars were squeezed together to fit in your hand. That is how tight and tiny the ball was! Scientists think that everything began expanding outward about 14 billion years ago. All the **matter** in the universe exploded out at once! That is why the event is called the Big Bang.

When all the **matter** in the ball began moving out, it was very hot. It was hotter than even the hottest star. Everything was moving so fast as it expanded that nothing could stick together. It was too hot and fast for anything to be like what it is today. There were no galaxies, no stars, no planets, and no people.

But over time the **matter** began to cool. As the **matter** cooled and stopped moving so fast, gravity was able to hold little bits of **matter** together in **spheres**. These little **spheres**, with the help of gravity, came together and became the first stars and galaxies. Over billions of years of **matter** moving and growing, the universe became the way it looks today. The sun and planets in our solar system formed about four billion years ago.

*All **matter** in the universe expanded out from one tiny point.*

Scientists are continuing to look into space for more clues about the Big Bang. There is still a lot to learn about the early universe. Scientists sometimes make minor changes to the **Big Bang Theory** to match what they have learned. It is amazing to think how old our solar system is and that scientists are still trying to find out how it all started!

This satellite helped scientists learn more about the early universe.

What's in Our Universe?

Glossary for *What's in Our Universe?*

A

African-American studies—the study of the history, culture, and politics of African-Americans, Americans who have ancestors from Africa

Andromeda Galaxy—the spiral galaxy that is closest to the Milky Way Galaxy

Apollo 11—a rocket ship that took three American astronauts to the moon in 1969

asteroid—a space rock, smaller than a planet, that orbits the sun (**asteroids**)

asteroid belt—an area between Mars and Jupiter where thousands of asteroids orbit around the sun in a shape like a belt

astronaut—a person who travels into outer space

astronomer—a scientist who studies stars, planets, and outer space (**astronomers**)

astrophysicist—a scientist who studies the physical characteristics of heavenly bodies (**astrophysicists**)

atmosphere—an invisible, protective blanket of air around Earth and other heavenly bodies

attraction—when things are drawn to move closer together

axis—an imaginary straight line through the middle of an object, around which that object spins

B

Big Bang Theory—a scientific explanation of how the universe began

billion—a very large number (**billions**)

booster rocket—one of two parts of a space shuttle that helps launch it into space by overcoming gravity (**booster rockets**)

C

chemical engineering—a field of study in which scientists use their knowledge of chemistry and how things in the natural world are made and interact

comet—a frozen ball of dust and ice that travels through outer space (**comets**)

What's in Our Universe?

constellation—stars that form a pattern or shape that looks like such things as a person, an object, or an animal as seen from Earth (**constellations**)

courage—bravery

E

eclipse—the blocking of the light from the sun by another heavenly body (**eclipses**)

Endeavour—a NASA space shuttle

especially—very much, particularly

exploration—the study of unknown places or things

G

galaxy—a very large cluster of billions of stars, dust, and gas held together by gravity and separated from other star systems by a large amount of space (**galaxies**)

gas giant—one of the large outer planets, Jupiter, Saturn, Uranus, and Neptune, that is composed of mainly hydrogen gas (**gas giants**)

gravity—a force that pulls things toward one another

H

Halley's Comet—a famous comet named for British scientist Edmund Halley that is visible from Earth with the naked eye every 76 years

health care—the prevention or treatment of illnesses by trained medical specialists

Hubble Telescope—a large telescope that collects information in space; It was carried into space in 1990 and will be there until 2014.

hydrogen—the most common gas in the universe, which is lighter than air and easily catches fire

I

imagine—to pretend

international—involving more than one country

L

launch—to send a rocket into outer space (**launched**)

M

manned—carrying and operated by people

matter—the stuff everything in the universe is made of; anything that takes up space

meteor—a piece of rock that burns very brightly when it enters Earth's atmosphere from space, also called a shooting star (**meteors**)

meteorite—a meteor that does not fully burn up in Earth's atmosphere and falls to Earth

meteoroid—a space rock, smaller than an asteroid, that orbits the sun (**meteoroids**)

Milky Way Galaxy—the galaxy that contains Earth and the solar system in which it lies

N

naked eye—your eye

NASA—National Aeronautics and Space Administration; an organization in the United States that directs space travel and research

O

observatory—a place used to observe the sun, moon, stars, and outer space (**observatories**)

orbit—the curved path something in space takes around another object in space; Planets move in an orbit around the sun. (**orbiting**)

P

Peace Corps—a group of American volunteers who carry out projects in other countries to help improve the lives of people living there

planet—a round object in space that orbits a star (**planets**)

Polaris—the North Star; the brightest star at the end of the handle of the Ursa Minor/Little Dipper that stays in the same place in the night sky all year long

probe—a tool used to explore something, such as outer space (**probes**)

R

research—the kind of equipment used to collect information through experiments

eusable—when something can be used more than once

rotate—to turn about an axis or a center (**rotating, rotates, rotation**)

S

satellite—a natural or man-made object that orbits a planet or smaller object (**satellites**)

shuttle—to go back and forth from one place to the next (**shuttled**)

solar system—the sun, other bodies like asteroids and meteors, and the planets that orbit the sun

space shuttle—a manned spacecraft used for exploration

space station—a manned satellite that is made to be in outer space for a long period of time

sphere—an object shaped like a ball (**spheres**)

T

theory—a suggested explanation for why something happens (**theories**)

tilted—slanted or tipped to one side

U

unmanned—not carrying people

Ursa Major—the constellation named by Ptolemy that is also called Big Bear; It includes the Big Dipper.

Ursa Minor—the constellation made of seven stars named by Ptolemy that is also called Little Bear; It is the Little Dipper.

V

volunteer—a person who willingly performs a service without getting paid

W

weightlessness—to have little or no weight